Stress Less
1 and 2 Combo
Coloring Book

60 Intricate detail full page mandalas for coloring in

For relaxation and stress relief

By Artist
Dwyanna Stoltzfus

Join the Fun!!

Share your colored pages!!

You are invited to color the pages
From this and all publications by
Dwyanna Stoltzfus. Then scan and post
Your colored creations in
Coloring with Dwyanna
Adult Coloring Group
On facebook
https://web.facebook.com/groups/1519357628356169/?_rdr
Join Coloring with Dwyanna Coloring Group,
And have fun sharing your colored pages
And meeting new coloring friends.
Members of the group will also have access
To free coloring pages.
You are welcome to share your colored pages on
Any social network, make sure to mention the title of
The book and the author/artist name.
Uncolored images may not be shared.

Check out my blog at:

coloringwithdwyanna.blogspot.com

PDF Printable coloring pages available
On Etsy at

https://www.etsy.com/people/dwyannastoltzfus

Follow Dwyanna's art on facebook at
Oodles of Doodles Designs –
Adult Coloring Books by
Dwyanna Stoltzfus

https://web.facebook.com/Oodles-of-Doodles-Designs-Adult-Coloring-Books-by-Dwyanna-Stoltzfus-743502922387046/

About:

Get ready to color 60 fantastic stress relieving patterns by Artist Dwyanna Stoltzfus.

In this adult coloring book you will find 60 beautiful illustrations, printed one per page.

A collection of wonderful detailed patterns that relax you

and melt away stress and tension as you color.

This book is a combo book of all the patterns in

Stress Less 1 and Stress Less 2 Books.

You can use this coloring book to help you relax and unwind after a long day.

Or you can use it just for fun. You can color the designs simply or add depth and creativity by shading and highlighting.

Crayons are not recommended for the intricate designs but may be used on some of the pages.

You can also color with fine tip markers, gel pens, and colored pencils.

Enjoy the experience of coloring!!

But most of all relax and have fun!!

Coloring tips:

If you desire to add depth to your coloring you can shade with colored pencils.

Use dark colors around edges and into the peaks. Blend in light colors for the

middle and more open spaces. You can use black to darken areas,

and white to lighten and brighten areas.

Acknowledgments

Thank You to my family for all your support
of my art and this project.
I could not have done it without you!!

Thank You God for the gift and love
Of art and drawing!!

Stress Less 2 Coloring Book

30 Intricate detail full page mandalas for coloring in

for relaxation and stress relief

By Artist

Dwyanna Stoltzfus

www.ingramcontent.com/pod-product-compliance
Lightning Source LLC
Chambersburg PA
CBHW081729220526
45468CB00008B/2026